Life Cycles
Butterflies and Moths

Julie K. Lundgren

Rourke
Educational Media

rourkeeducationalmedia.com

www.rourkeeducationalmedia.com

Photo credits: Cover © Mau Horng, Chris Turner, Lori Skelton, Kati Molin; Title Page © Kati Molin; Contents © Luna Vandoorne, Cathy Keifer, EtiAmmos; Page 4 © Chekaramit; Page 5 © Ambient Ideas; Page 6 © Elizabeth Spencer; Page 7 © Chekaramit, Louis Bourgeois; Page 8 © Maryunin Yury Vasilevich; Page 9 © limpid; Page 10 © Mau Horng; Page 11 © Luna Vandoorne; Page 12/13 © Cathy Keifer; Page 14 © Ianaré Sévi; Page 15 © Dr. Morley Read, Chekaramit; Page 16 © Andy Heyward; Page 17 © Cathy Keifer, EtiAmmos; Page 18 © Jens Stolt, Yenyu Shih, Michael C. Gray; Page 19 © Laurie Barr; Page 21 © nikkytok, Ambient Ideas; Page 22 © Luna Vandoorne, Cathy Keifer, Andy Heyward, limpid

Editor: Jeanne Sturm

Cover and page design by Nicola Stratford, bdpublishing.com

Library of Congress Cataloging-in-Publication Data

Lundgren, Julie K.
 Butterflies and moths / Julie K. Lundgren.
     p. cm. -- (Life cycles)
 Includes bibliographical references and index.
 ISBN 978-1-61590-308-5 (Hard Cover) (alk. paper)
 ISBN 978-1-61590-547-8 (Soft Cover)
 1. Butterflies--Life cycles--Juvenile literature. 2. Moths--Life cycles--Juvenile literature. I. Title.
 QL544.2.L86 2011
 595.78'9--dc22
                                    2010009024

Rourke Educational Media
Printed in the United States of America,
North Mankato, Minnesota

rourkeeducationalmedia.com
customerservice@rourkeeducationalmedia.com • PO Box 643328 Vero Beach, Florida 32964

Table of Contents

Insect Beauties

Butterflies and moths belong to the insect group of animals. They have bodies divided into three sections called the head, **thorax**, and **abdomen**. The head has eyes and **antennae**. Wings and feet attach to the thorax.

Hawk moth

Like most other insects, butterflies and moths have six legs and two pairs of wings.

Monarch butterfly

antennae

thorax

abdomen

DID YOU KNOW?

A butterfly or moth smells with its antennae and tastes with its feet.

Butterflies and moths differ in several ways.

	Moth	Butterfly
Antennae	Simple or fuzzy, no clubs	Usually plain, with clubbed ends
Most active time of day	Dawn, dusk, or night	Day
Wing Position at Rest	Flat, open	Straight up, together
Colors	Usually dull, with patterns that help them blend in	Colorful, with bold patterns
Body Shape	Chunkier	Slender

Moth antennae can be straight or feathery, but have no end clubs.

Blood-vein moth

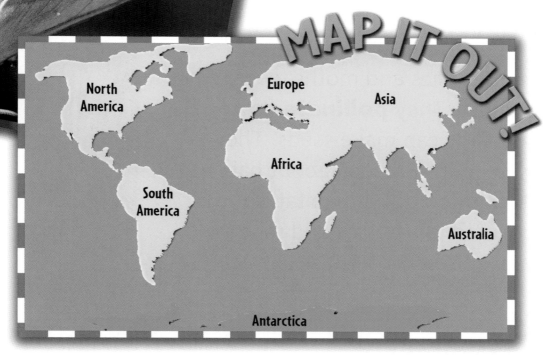

North America

Europe

Asia

Africa

South America

Australia

Antarctica

Butterflies and moths live on every continent but Antarctica.

Butterfly antennae have little clubs, or bumps, on the ends.

Monarch butterfly

DID YOU KNOW?

Scientists think 12,000 to 15,000 kinds of butterflies and 150,000 to 250,000 kinds of moths live on Earth. More await discovery!

Butterflies and moths feed other animals. They **pollinate** flowers so plants can make seeds. They give people an idea about habitat health, too. If the habitat is too polluted, butterflies and moths leave or die.

A dark clouded yellow butterfly finds a tasty lunch inside a knautia flower.

Many flowers depend on butterflies, like this common jay butterfly, for pollination.

Egg-cellent Start

All living things have a life cycle. They begin life, grow, **reproduce**, and then die. The cycle happens again and again. Insects like butterflies and moths change forms as they go through their life cycle. They begin as tiny eggs.

Butterflies and moths may lay round, oval, bumpy, smooth, or striped eggs. Each kind of butterfly or moth lays eggs with a particular shape, color, and pattern.

Depending on the kind, butterflies and moths may lay many eggs together or just one egg on each plant or leaf.

DID YOU KNOW?

Butterflies and moths lay eggs on plants their caterpillars like to eat. Monarchs lay eggs on milkweed.

Eating Machines

After 3 to 10 days, the eggs hatch and the second stage of life begins. A caterpillar, or larva, grows quickly. It sheds its skin, or molts, when its skin gets too tight. Caterpillars molt several times.

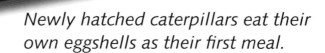

Newly hatched caterpillars eat their own eggshells as their first meal.

New skin gives the monarch caterpillars growing room.

Cycle Snapshot

The time between each molt is called an instar. Monarch butterflies have five instars.

Animals enjoy eating caterpillars. How do any survive? Color forms one defense. Bold colors and patterns often signal a warning that the caterpillars contain poison. Green caterpillars blend into their surroundings.

Caterpillars eat night and day. Their bodies store the energy they get from food. They must gather enough energy for the changes to come.

Some caterpillars, like the giant swallowtail, look like lumps of bird droppings.

The saturniid moth caterpillar has spikes for protection.

Cycle Snapshot

A monarch lives as a caterpillar for about two weeks.

The hawk moth caterpillar safely eats poisonous plants and stores the poison in its body. Its stripes remind birds to stay away.

15

Changes

Fully grown caterpillars search for a safe place to begin the **pupa** stage. After attaching their tails to a branch or leaf, butterfly caterpillars molt one last time, revealing the **chrysalis**. Many moths spin silk **cocoons** around themselves. Others form a hard shell and rest on the ground.

The monarch butterfly forms a chrysalis that looks like hanging fruit.

The monarch caterpillar forms its chrysalis in several steps, beginning with a hook that looks like the letter J.

DID YOU KNOW?

An Atlas Moth has wings 10 to 12 inches (25 to 30 centimeters) from tip to tip.

Many kinds of moth caterpillars, like lappet moths, form cocoons in which to change to adults.

Inside the chrysalis or cocoon, the caterpillar's body changes. Much of it breaks down into a rich soup that provides food for the developing adult.

After the chrysalis breaks open, the new butterfly rests several hours. It must dry its wet wings before it can fly.

Chrysalises come in many colors and patterns.

A monarch butterfly spends about 12-14 days in its chrysalis before coming out as an adult butterfly.

Wonderful Wings

Many butterflies and moths sip flower nectar for energy; while others dine on moist, rotting fruit, tree sap, or animal waste. They find partners and lay eggs to begin the life cycle again. Near summer's end, some kinds **migrate** to warm wintering grounds.

Zoos and nature centers often plant gardens especially for butterflies and moths. The gardens contain flowering plants that butterflies, moths, and their caterpillars like. Plant a few favorites in your yard!

Cycle Snapshot

Female butterflies and moths lay several hundred eggs in their lifetime. Few become adults, as little as one or two out of every 100 eggs laid.

Blue morpho butterflies, like other adult butterflies, cannot chew. They drink their food instead.

DID YOU KNOW?

Monarch butterflies migrate south in the fall. Monarchs return each spring to lay eggs.

21

Life Cycle Round-up

1 Butterflies and moths begin as eggs.

4 Adults come out to begin the cycle again.

2 A caterpillar, or larva, hatches, eats, grows, and molts several times.

3 It then forms a chrysalis or cocoon.

Glossary

abdomen (AB-duh-muhn): the last section of an insect, behind the thorax

antennae (an-TEN-ay): the two parts on the head of a butterfly or moth that sense smells

chrysalis (KRISS-uh-liss): the special protective shell in which a butterfly pupa changes to an adult

cocoons (KAH-koonz): the woven, protective coverings in which moth caterpillars change to adults

migrate (MYE-grate): move from one area to another according to the seasons

pollinate (POL-uh-nate): move plant pollen from one flower to another, allowing seeds to develop

pupa (PYOO-puh): the stage of development between a caterpillar and an adult

reproduce (ree-proh-DOOS): make more of something

thorax (THOR-aks): the body section located between the head and abdomen

Index

Websites to Visit

www.butterfliesandmoths.org/

www.flmnh.ufl.edu/butterflies/

www.kidsbutterfly.org/

www.fs.fed.us/monarchbutterfly/index.shtml

www.monarchwatch.org/biology/cycle1.htm

www.thebutterflysite.com/

About the Author

Julie K. Lundgren grew up near Lake Superior where she reveled in mucking about in the woods, picking berries, and expanding her rock collection. Her appetite for learning about nature led her to a degree in biology from the University of Minnesota. She currently lives in Minnesota with her husband and two sons.

NUTRITIOUS & DELICIOUS™

Enjoy
Healthy Eating
with
ActiFry®

T-fal®

Ellie Krieger - MS, RD
Registered Dietitian
New York Times Best Selling Author, Food Network Host
Former Adjunct Professor New York University Department of
Nutrition, Food Studies and Public Health

" Most people think the words delicious and healthy can't be used in the same sentence. I can hardly blame them since so many foods billed as good-for-you are so disappointing taste-wise. Happily, as a born food lover and credentialed nutritionist, I have found a way to celebrate and enjoy fabulous food in a healthier way. Food is such a wonderful part of life, in my world there is no fear or guilt about it, only pleasure and balance.

Like you I crave food that's bursting with flavor and aroma, food that tempts you and leaves you satisfied-food that not only delights your taste buds but also benefits the rest of your body. Guess what? You can have it all! That is something I have been helping people achieve for years now, through my books, TV shows, magazine articles and websites.

We all know how important it is to the whole family's well-being to establish healthy eating habits at home. But as a busy working mom, I understand first hand how challenging it can be to put good food on the table that everyone enjoys. Sometimes all you need are the right tools to make it happen. ActiFry is one of those helpful tools.

When I was introduced to ActiFry it was wow at first sight. French fries have always been one of my favorite indulgences, and since "never" is not in my food vocabulary, I would splurge on them once in a while. But when I learned that with ActiFry I could have crispy, satisfying fries, made nearly effortlessly with just a tablespoonful of healthy oil, I knew it would become my favorite kitchen tool. Now I can feel good about serving fries at home and my daughter, like every other kid, loves them. Beyond fries, I am excited and amazed about all the other delectable dishes I can make easily and healthfully in the ActiFry. I am thrilled to be able to share them with you here. "

Contents

NUTRITIOUS & DELICIOUS™

NUTRITIOUS & DELICIOUS™

Innovating To

Healthy eating is not just about ingredients but bringing the best out of the foods we cook. And because not all cooking appliances are created equal, T-fal has developed Nutritious & Delicious, a range of ingenious culinary appliances that help home cooks to cook food in ways that preserve nutritional integrity and allow the taste of ingredients to be fully appreciated.

✛ Proven Results

T-fal is proud to be at the forefront of culinary research and development. We invest in innovation to develop unique cooking solutions that deliver nutritional advantages, which are validated by scientific studies.

✛ Made for You

T-fal understands that although busy lifestyles require fast and easy cooking techniques, many consumers want to improve their general health.

T-fal has always provided practical solutions in the kitchen and now our focus is to make nutritious and tasty meals accessible to everyone.

Improve Health

The pleasure of eating with ActiFry

ActiFry, part of the **T-fal** Nutritious & Delicious appliance line, can help you to achieve dietary balance without sacrificing culinary pleasure.

At its best, eating should be a pleasurable experience, one that combines sharing food and friendship while providing the nourishment that is vital to maintain general good health and well-being.

✚ Well-being and healthy food

Studies have repeatedly shown that healthy eating plays a key role in the prevention of serious conditions such as heart disease, diabetes, obesity and even some cancers. Following a healthy diet can also help you and your loved ones to stay fit by providing the nutrients needed to fuel activity.

✚ A revolutionary appliance

Every ActiFry recipe meets MyPyramid guidelines and uses unique preparation techniques that control fat content. A team of professional home economists and nutritionists created and tested this roster of great tasting, easily prepared recipes to help you maintain a balanced diet.

✚ A balanced diet without compromising on taste

Using ActiFry, you'll prepare delicious, nutritious meals with less added fat. When used with our nutritionally analyzed recipes, ActiFry is a terrific tool that can help you to enjoy your meals while reducing your risk of heart disease and excess weight gain.

✚ A sophisticated technology

ActiFry's unique cooking method uses sophisticated technology to create lower fat versions of the foods we all love including family favorites such as French fries! This versatile appliance can also be used to cook healthy entrées prepared with lean meat, poultry and fish as well as nutritious vegetable side dishes and yummy fruit desserts.

5

NUTRITIOUS & DELICIOUS™

Eating enhances a

Maintaining a healthy diet requires eating well regularly.

Since planning ahead can ensure that you eat well all week, we've included helpful menu plans (see pages 18 to 21) that incorporate a variety of recipes from this booklet. Using ActiFry with these plans and recipes, you'll enjoy delicious and nutritious meals that are fast and easy to prepare!

 **Breakfast**

Considered by many health experts as the most important meal, a balanced breakfast refuels the body with necessary nutrients to provide energy after a night of fasting. Choosing breakfast options that include slowly released energy sources such as complex carbohydrates and protein leads to lasting satisfaction and reduces cravings for mid-morning snacks.

A balanced breakfast includes:
- One to two servings of complex carbohydrates such as whole grain cereals or breads.
- A serving of fruits or vegetables such as oranges, berries, bananas, apples, spinach, tomatoes or 100% fruit or vegetable juice.

- A protein source such as eggs, low-fat dairy products, nuts or lean meats.

 Lunch

Busy schedules and workday demands can interfere with eating a proper lunch. Studies show that eating a nutritious lunch can improve productivity and prevent splurging later in the day. A balanced lunch contains elements from all food groups.

 Dinner

Since the evening meal is often a time to sit down and savor your food, it's a perfect opportunity to

use the delicious recipes in this booklet. Make old favorites with healthy new benefits; add variety by trying new recipes; or, use our ideas as a springboard for new ways to use your ActiFry.

At the same time, keep portion control in mind. Review MyPyramid to assess the servings you've consumed throughout the day. This review will help you to adjust your dinner menu so that you consume the appropriate amount and variety of foods for your age, weight and sex.

healthy meals, healthy lifestyle!

NUTRITIOUS & DELICIOUS™

Making Nutritious Choices

1 ActiFry is a valuable tool to control fat content because it uses a cooking method that reduces the amount of fat required for cooking and duplicates the flavors and textures of our favorite fried foods.

2 Eat whole grain foods that offer the body valuable nutrients including vitamins, minerals, antioxidants and fiber. Select from the wide variety of available grain products such as whole-wheat pastas and breads, barley, brown rice, oats and corn.

3 Drink low-fat milk or fortified soy beverages to supply the body essential calcium and vitamin D.

4 Make your protein choices leaner by trimming visible fat from pork and red meats, removing the skin from poultry or fish, or by frequently choosing meatless entrée options such as beans, lentils or tofu.

5 Include colorful vegetables such as dark green broccoli or spinach, bright orange carrots or sweet potatoes, red peppers and purple beets in your diet each day.

6 Add as little salt as possible during cooking and, whenever possible, buy products that are lower in sodium. Read the Nutrition Facts tables to check the sodium content of prepared products.

7 Include a small amount of unsaturated fat in your diet each day to provide essential fatty acids. Moderate servings of nuts, seeds, vegetable oils and fatty fish (such as salmon, sardines and trout) are nutritious sources of essential fats.

8 Limit harmful saturated and trans fat in your diet by choosing lean meats, low-fat dairy products and non-hydrogenated spreads.

9 Keep hydrated by drinking water, low-fat milk, 100% fruit juices and other caffeine-free beverages throughout the day. Calorie-free water is the ideal thirst-quenching choice.

10 Above all, eat a wide variety of foods in appropriate portion sizes.

Eating well with MyPyramid

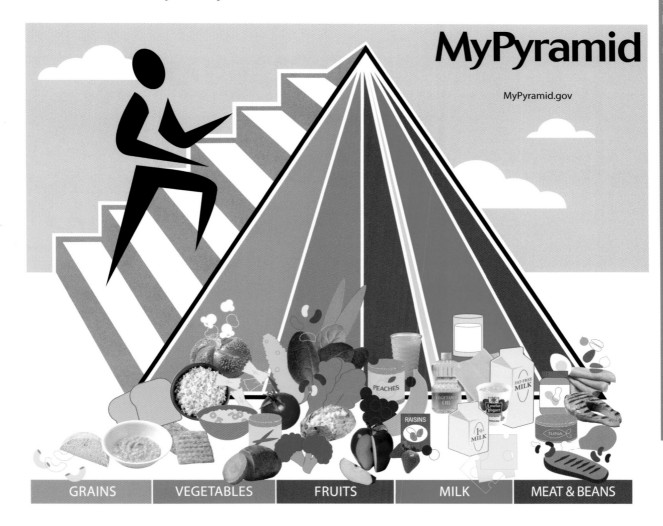

MyPyramid

MyPyramid.gov

GRAINS | VEGETABLES | FRUITS | MILK | MEAT & BEANS

NUTRITIOUS & DELICIOUS™

GRAINS	VEGETABLES	FRUITS	MILK	MEAT & BEANS
Make half your grains whole	Vary your veggies	Focus on fruits	Get your calcium-rich foods	Go lean with protein
Eat at least 3 oz. of whole-grain cereals, breads, crackers, rice, or pasta every day

1 oz. is about 1 slice of bread, about 1 cup of breakfast cereal, or ½ cup of cooked rice, cereal, or pasta | Eat more dark-green veggies like broccoli, spinach, and other dark leafy greens

Eat more orange vegetables like carrots and sweetpotatoes

Eat more dry beans and peas like pinto beans, kidney beans, and lentils | Eat a variety of fruit

Choose fresh, frozen, canned, or dried fruit

Go easy on fruit juices | Go low-fat or fat-free when you choose milk, yogurt, and other milk products

If you don't or can't consume milk, choose lactose-free products or other calcium sources such as fortified foods and beverages | Choose low-fat or lean meats and poultry

Bake it, broil it, or grill it

Vary your protein routine — choose more fish, beans, peas, nuts, and seeds |

For a 2,000-calorie diet, you need the amounts below from each food group. To find the amounts that are right for you, go to MyPyramid.gov.

Eat 6 oz. every day	Eat 2½ cups every day	Eat 2 cups every day	Get 3 cups every day; for kids aged 2 to 8, it's 2	Eat 5½ oz. every day

Find your balance between food and physical activity

- Be sure to stay within your daily calorie needs.
- Be physically active for at least 30 minutes most days of the week.
- About 60 minutes a day of physical activity may be needed to prevent weight gain.
- For sustaining weight loss, at least 60 to 90 minutes a day of physical activity may be required.
- Children and teenagers should be physically active for 60 minutes every day, or most days.

Know the limits on fats, sugars, and salt (sodium)

- Make most of your fat sources from fish, nuts, and vegetable oils.
- Limit solid fats like butter, stick margarine, shortening, and lard, as well as foods that contain these.
- Check the Nutrition Facts label to keep saturated fats, trans fats, and sodium low.
- Choose food and beverages low in added sugars. Added sugars contribute calories with few, if any, nutrients.

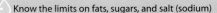

MyPyramid.gov
STEPS TO A HEALTHIER YOU

U.S. Department of Agriculture
Center for Nutrition Policy and Promotion
March 2005
CNPP-15

USDA

USDA Food Guide

Daily Amount of Food From Each Group (vegetable subgroup amounts are per week)						
Calorie Level	1,000	1,200	1,400	1,600	1,800	2,000
Food Group	Food group amounts shown in cup (c) or ounce-equivalents (oz-eq), with number of servings (srv) in parentheses when it differs from the other units. See note for quantity equivalents for foods in each group. Oils are shown in grams (g).					
Fruits	1 c (2 srv)	1 c (2 srv)	1.5 c (3 srv)	1.5 c (3 srv)	1.5 c (3 srv)	2 c (4 srv)
Vegetables	1 c (2 srv)	1.5 c (3 srv)	1.5 c (3 srv)	2 c (4 srv)	2.5 c (5 srv)	2.5 c (5 srv)
Dark green veg.	1 c/wk	1.5 c/wk	1.5 c/wk	2 c/wk	3 c/wk	3 c/wk
Orange veg.	.5 c/wk	1 c/wk	1 c/wk	1.5 c/wk	2 c/wk	2 c/wk
Legumes	.5 c/wk	1 c/wk	1 c/wk	2.5 c/wk	3 c/wk	3 c/wk
Starchy veg.	1.5 c/wk	2.5 c/wk	2.5 c/wk	2.5 c/wk	3 c/wk	3 c/wk
Other veg.	4 c/wk	4.5 c/wk	4.5 c/wk	5.5 c/wk	6.5 c/wk	6.5 c/wk
Grains	3 oz-eq	4 oz-eq	5 oz-eq	5 oz-eq	6 oz-eq	6 oz-eq
Whole grains	1.5	2	2.5	3	3	3
Other grains	1.5	2	2.5	2	3	3
Lean meat and beans	2 oz-eq	3 oz-eq	4 oz-eq	5 oz-eq	5 oz-eq	5.5 oz-eq
Milk	2 c	2 c	2 c	3 c	3 c	3 c
Oils	15 g	17 g	17 g	22 g	24 g	27 g
Discretionary calorie allowance	165	171	171	132	195	267

Calorie Level	2,200	2,400	2,600	2,800	3,000	3,200
Fruits	2 c (4 srv)	2 c (4 srv)	2 c (4 srv)	2.5 c (5 srv)	2.5 c (5 srv)	2.5 c (5 srv)
Vegetables	3 c (6 srv)	3 c (6 srv)	3.5 c (7 srv)	3.5 c (7 srv)	4 c (8 srv)	4 c (8 srv)
Dark green veg.	3 c/wk	3 c/wk	3 c/wk	3 c/wk	3 c/wk	3 c/wk
Orange veg.	2 c/wk	2 c/wk	2.5 c/wk	2.5 c/wk	2.5 c/wk	2.5 c/wk
Legumes	3 c/wk	3 c/wk	3.5 c/wk	3.5 c/wk	3.5 c/wk	3.5 c/wk
Starchy veg.	6 c/wk	6 c/wk	7 c/wk	7 c/wk	9 c/wk	9 c/wk
Other veg.	7 c/wk	7 c/wk	8.5 c/wk	8.5 c/wk	10 c/wk	10 c/wk
Grains	7 oz-eq	8 oz-eq	9 oz-eq	10 oz-eq	10 oz-eq	10 oz-eq
Whole grains	3.5	4	4.5	5	5	5
Other grains	3.5	4	4.5	5	5	5
Lean meat and beans	6 oz-eq	6.5 oz-eq	6.5 oz-eq	7 oz-eq	7 oz-eq	7 oz-eq
Milk	3 c	3 c	3 c	3 c	3 c	3 c
Oils	29 g	31 g	34 g	36 g	44 g	51 g
Discretionary calorie allowance	290	362	410	426	512	648

EATING HEALTHY MEALS, ENHANCES A HEALTHY LIFESTYLE!

Potatoes: A nutritious Choice

Although universally loved, potatoes have a bad nutritional reputation with dieters. The problem lies in the fact that so many of our favorite potato preparations are cooked and served in ways that add calories.

Considered on their own, potatoes are low fat vegetables that contain vitamin C, potassium, folate, fiber and other important nutrients including B vitamins.

Potato lovers looking to avoid fat can incorporate potatoes into a healthy lifestyle:

- Use ActiFry to make crispy and delicious potato side dishes.
- Put away your peeler. When eaten with the skin, a medium potato contains three grams of fiber. A diet rich in fiber is linked with a reduced risk of heart disease digestive health. Additionally, fiber may aid in weight loss by reducing the urge to snack.
- Choose potato recipes that include herbs and spices so it isn't necessary to add butter and salt at the table.

Potato Questions & Answers

What kind of potato is best for ActiFry cooking?

ActiFry can be used to cook many different types of potatoes:

- Halved or quartered baby new potatoes develop an oven-roasted texture when cooked in ActiFry.
- Russets and other high starch baking potatoes are ideal choices for homemade French fries.
- Yukon gold potatoes have the texture needed to make thicker, wedge-shaped fries.
- Even frozen French fries are appropriate for use in ActiFry.

How should I store fresh potatoes to retain nutrients, flavor and texture?

Potatoes should be stored in a dark, cool, dry and well-ventilated cupboard. If you buy potatoes wrapped or bagged in plastic, remove them from the packaging before storing.

How should I prepare potatoes to be cooked in ActiFry?

- If leaving skin on potatoes, wash well and use a paring knife to remove eyes and surface blemishes before preparing potatoes as specified in the recipe.

- Uniformity is important when cooking in ActiFry so be sure that potatoes cut for French fries are an even width and not too thick (our professional recipe testers recommend fries be less than ½ inch thick on all sides.). When making other potato recipes, cut the potatoes into chunks of similar size. Avoid cutting wedges with pointy ends, which can fracture and crumble during cooking.
- Rinse prepared, raw potatoes to be cooked in ActiFry in cold water to remove surface starch; drain well and pat completely dry on kitchen or paper towels.

13

All diets need to include some fat. The body requires fat to generate warmth and energy, to absorb fat-soluble vitamins and as a source of essential fatty acids.

That said, managing fat intake is one of the most important aspects of creating a healthy eating plan.

Diets very high in fat, especially saturated fat, are often linked with weight gain and unhealthy blood cholesterol levels. Health experts recommend that you limit total fat intake to no more than 35 % of your total daily caloric intake.

Saturated fats

Saturated fats are typically solid at room temperature and are found in foods such as red meats, full-fat dairy products and butter. Saturated fats have been shown to raise the "bad" LDL (low density lipoprotein) cholesterol in the bloodstream, increasing the risk of heart attack and stroke.

Trans fats

The majority of trans fats are produced when liquid vegetable oils are commercially hydrogenated into a solid form; however, some trans fats occur naturally in dairy and meat products. Trans fats are considered more harmful than saturated fats because while they raise LDL cholesterol, they also decrease "good" HDL (high density lipoprotein) cholesterol. This combined effect increase the risk of cardio-vascular disease. Manufacturers are required to list trans fat content on Nutrition Facts tables.

Many manufacturers are striving to eliminate trans fats entirely from their processed food products.

Polyunsaturated fats

A moderate amount of polyunsaturated fats is required to provide essential fatty acids that cannot be produced by our bodies. Essential fatty acids play a crucial role in brain function, proper growth and development and reducing inflammation.

perspective on fat

Choosing oil for the ActiFry

- Many types of oils can be used in the ActiFry to add flavor and character to your recipes.
- For higher monounsaturated and Omega-3 content use oils such as olive, canola and safflower oils.

(Note: Canola was the reference oil used during the testing of the recipes in this booklet.)

- Less refined or aromatic oils such as extra virgin olive oil and toasted sesame seed oil are best added at the end of ActiFry cooking as flavor accents.

Omega 3 fatty acids

- Studies have shown that Omega 3 fatty acids can be helpful in treating chronic diseases such as heart disease, diabetes, arthritis, osteoporosis, depression and macular degeneration.
- ALA (Alpha-linolenic acid) Omega 3 cannot be made by the body but is necessary for maintaining good health. It is found in fish, flaxseed, walnuts, pumpkin seeds and vegetable oils such as canola and soybean.
- The body can convert ALA consumed in the diet into DHA (docosahexaenoic acid) and EPA (eicosapentaenoic acid), two forms of Omega 3's readily utilized by the body.

- DHA and EPA can also be attained as part of a well-planned diet and are primarily found in cold-water fish such as salmon, tuna, mackerel, sardines and herring.

Omega 6 fatty acids

- Although Omega 6 fatty acids cannot be produced by the body, they are prevalent in processed foods because many oils used in food manufacturing (such as sunflower, safflower, corn and sesame) are rich in this essential fatty acid.

- Diets that emphasize whole grains, fresh fruits and vegetables, fish, and healthy oils, like olive and canola, naturally provide an appropriate balance of these essential fats.

Monounsaturated fats

Monounsaturated fats are found in avocados, almonds and cooking oils such as canola, olive and peanut. When consumed instead of saturated fats, monounsaturated fats raise HDL cholesterol levels in the blood, reducing the risk of diseases associated with high blood cholesterol, namely heart disease and stroke.

Gourmet Cuisine

Prepare classic French fries just the way you like them!

Thanks to our patented technology, French fries are crispy on the outside and tender inside.

How does it work? The ActiFry has a stirring paddle that gently distributes a small amount of oil over the potatoes while hot, forced air creates a delicious French fry. All you need to do is combine potatoes, oil and herbs, spices or other seasonings and let ActiFry do the rest!

Treat your family without guilt!

A ¼ lb portion of fries prepared using ActiFry's cooking method contains only 3 % fat!*

A little goes a long way :

1 tablespoon of oil is all you need!

Add one ActiFry measuring spoon filled with oil to 2 lbs potatoes to make classic French fries!

Using the supplied ActiFry measuring spoon ensures perfect results every time.

Mix it Up!

Since all kinds of oils work in the ActiFry, you can experiment with a variety of flavors each time you make French fries or other ActiFry dishes. Some oils (see page 15) also contain the essential fatty acids your body needs for good health.

Fabulous with Frozen

Many frozen vegetables options are a good alternative to fresh products especially in winter. Not only are frozen products often less expensive than fresh, but the flash-freezing process can lock in nutrients that are lost when products are trucked and stored.

*Based on SEB IS-SUR-TILLE laboratory test reports #'s RE 06-0084 & RE 06-0133. Re: 1000 g fresh potato french fries (13 mm x 13 mm), peeled, washed and cooked to 55 % weight loss.

with ActiFry

Love your ActiFry!

Use these cooking tips and tricks to maximize your enjoyment of this innovative new appliance:

- To prevent over-seasoning, add salt to fries and potato wedges just before serving rather than during preparation or cooking.

- When adding dried herbs and spices to ActiFry, blend them with some oil or liquid. Sprinkling dry seasonings directly into the cooking chamber will result in poor flavor distribution since the hot air system will blow these dry ingredients around.

- Use grated or finely chopped garlic instead of crushed to prevent the garlic from sticking to the central paddle.

- Although vividly colored spices may slightly stain the paddle and other parts of the appliance, this color change will not affect the results of future recipes.

- Never fill the ActiFry beyond the maximum food level mark indicated on the pan.

- High-liquid recipes such as soups or liquid sauces are not recommended for this appliance; using too much liquid may cause messy overflow into the base of the unit.

- When preparing meat and poultry dishes, stop the appliance and stir the pan contents once or twice during cooking so that the food on top does not dry out and to ensure that the cooking juices thicken evenly.

- Chop vegetables to be cooked in the ActiFry into equal, bite-sized sized shapes to ensure that they cook evenly and thoroughly.

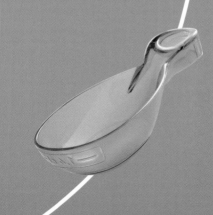

Examples of

Recipes included in the booklet.

	Sunday	Monday	Tuesday
Breakfast	Whole grain pancakes topped with Glazed Apple Wedges (p82) Low fat milk	Egg white omelet with spinach and diced tomatoes Whole grain toast Orange juice	Whole grain cereal with low fat milk and banana slices
Lunch	Grilled Salmon over mixed green salad Whole grain roll	Crab and Corn Chowder Whole grain roll Mixed Berry Compote (p80)	Spinach salad with chickpeas, feta cheese, tomato, mushrooms and red onion Whole grain breadsticks Apple slices with cinnamon
Dinner	Sesame beef with broccoli over brown rice (p52) Orange Wedges	Roasted Chicken Breast Potato Wedges with Herbs and Spices (p28) Sautéed spinach with garlic and olive oil Pear	Broiled pork tenderloin Rice Pilaf Steamed green beans Roasted Pineapple with Figs and Honey (p78)

balanced menus - week 1

Wednesday	Thursday	Friday	Saturday
Low fat yogurt with **Cherry-Pecan Granola** and fresh berries (p83)	Whole grain toast with peanut butter and all-fruit jam Apple slices Low fat milk	Oatmeal with walnuts and raisins Low fat milk	Smoked salmon, tomato slice, red onion and whipped cream cheese on Pumpernickel bread Orange wedges
Lean ham on whole grain bread with lettuce, tomato and mustard Celery and carrot sticks with **Blue Cheese Dip** (p40)	Hummus and vegetables in a whole wheat pita pocket Orange slices	Turkey with lettuce, tomato and avocado on a whole grain roll **Classic Crispy French Fries** (p24)	**Chipotle Beef Chili** (p56) Mixed green salad
Scallops and Asparagus Sauté Over brown rice (p63) Mixed green salad Melon slices	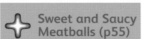 **Sweet and Saucy Meatballs** (p55) Steamed Brown Rice Spinach Salad with green apple slices and sunflower seeds Grapes	Broiled Flounder Fillet **Green Beans with Almonds and Parsley** (p70) Brown rice Fruit salad	Turkey burger with lettuce and tomato on whole grain roll **Sweet Potato Fries** (p27)

	Sunday	Monday	Tuesday
Breakfast	Poached or boiled egg on whole grain toast **Home Fries (p31)** Orange wedges	Oatmeal with sliced almonds and dried cherries Low fat milk	Whole grain cereal with fresh blueberries and low fat milk
Lunch	Chicken Noodle Soup Mixed Green Salad Whole grain crackers with reduced fat cheddar cheese	Salmon Salad in whole grain wrap with lettuce Low fat yogurt with sliced peaches	Whole wheat pita with hummus and vegetables Tomato and Cucumber Salad
Dinner	 **Sweet and Sour Pork Tenderloin** over brown rice **(p51)** Steamed broccoli Light vanilla ice cream or frozen yogurt	Grilled chicken breast Spaghetti with **Basil Pasta Sauce (p72)** Sauteed zucchini and onions Fruit Salad	**Turkey with 3 Peppers (p49)** Crusty whole grain Bread Melon Slices

 Recipes included in the booklet.

20

balanced menus - week 2

Wednesday	Thursday	Friday	Saturday
Whole grain toast with peanut butter Banana slices Low fat milk	Egg white omelet with spinach and diced tomatoes Whole grain toast Orange juice	Whole grain English muffin with peanut butter and all fruit jam Low fat milk	Cherry-Pecan Granola (p83) Low fat milk or yogurt
Tomato Soup Whole wheat tortilla grilled with shredded pepper jack cheese Apple	Romaine lettuce salad with shaves Parmesan Cheese and light Caesar Dressing with Grilled Shrimp Grapes	Lean roast beef with arugula, tomato, red onion and mustard on whole grain bread Peach	Spinach salad with grilled chicken and sliced almonds Whole grain roll Strawberries
Tuscan white beans with sausage (p50) Mixed green salad Orange wedges	Rotisserie Chicken Steamed Asparagus with Roasted Red Pepper Dip (p39) Low-fat rice Pudding	Butternut squash risotto (p73) Light vanilla ice cream or frozen yogurt with fresh berries	Baby New Potatoes with Garlic, Tomato and Shrimp (p61) Mixed green salad Peach slices

21

French Fries
and Potato Wedges

For the crispiest fries, it is essential to thoroughly dry the fries.

181 calories —— Nutrients / serving

[3 g total fat ~ 0 g saturated fat ~ 0 g trans fat ~ 0 mg cholesterol
34 g carbohydrates ~ 3 g fiber ~ 3 g protein ~ 249 mg sodium ~ 881 mg potassium]

Classic Crispy French Fries

SERVES **4** · PREPARATION **15** min · COOKING **30/40** min

1 ¾ lbs	baking potatoes such as Yukon gold
1 🥄	canola or olive oil
½ tsp	salt (approx.)

1   Peel the potatoes and cut into fries of equal thickness, no more than ⅔ inch in square thickness recommended. Rinse fries thoroughly in water; drain well. Use a clean kitchen towel to thoroughly dry the fries.

2   Place the fries in the ActiFry Pan. Drizzle evenly with the oil. Cook for 30 to 40 minutes or until the fries are golden and cooked through, (the cooking time will vary depending on the thickness of the fries and the variety of potato used). Season fries with salt (adjust to taste).

Variation   Substitute a 28 oz bag of frozen fries for the fresh potatoes with no added oil.

Nutritious

Leave the skins on the potatoes for additional fiber.
Excellent source of: Vitamin C.

Nutrients / serving —— **187 calories**

[7 g total fat ~ 1 g saturated fat ~ 0 g trans fat ~ 0 mg cholesterol
30 g carbohydrates ~ 2 g fiber ~ 4 g protein ~ 246 mg sodium ~ 686 mg potassium]

Paprika Fries

SERVES **4** · PREPARATION **15** min · COOKING **30/40** min

1 ¾ lbs	baking potatoes such as Yukon gold
½	paprika
2	vegetable oil
½ tsp	salt (approx.)

1 Peel the potatoes and cut into fries of equal thickness, no more than ⅔ inch in square thickness recommended. Rinse fries thoroughly in water; drain well. Use a clean kitchen towel to thoroughly dry the fries.

2 Place the fries in a bowl. Toss gently with the paprika and half of the oil to evenly coat the fries.

3 Transfer the fries to the ActiFry pan; drizzle evenly with the remaining oil. Cook for 30 to 40 minutes or until the fries are golden and cooked through, (the cooking time will vary depending on the thickness of the fries and the variety of potato used). Season fries with salt (adjust to taste).

Variation Toss the potatoes with any of your favorite seasoning blends such as Montreal steak spice, Tex Mex seasoning or garlic-herb blend.

25

200 calories _____ Nutrients / serving

[3.5 g total fat ~ 0.5 g saturated fat ~ 2.5 g monounsaturated fat ~ 0.5 g polyunsaturated fat
0 mg cholesterol ~ 38 g carbohydrates ~ 3 g fiber ~ 300 mg sodium]

✚ Nutritious

Excellent source of: Vitamin B6, Vitamin C, Manganese, Potassium. Good source of: Fiber, Thiamin, Niacin, Copper, Iron, Magnesium, Phosphorus.

Garlic Fries by Ellie Krieger

SERVES **4** · PREPARATION **10** min · COOKING **30/35** min

1 ¾ lbs	Russet potatoes, unpeeled
8	large cloves of garlic
1 	olive oil
½ tsp	salt, plus more to taste

1. Cut the potatoes into fries of equal thickness, about ½ inch square. Rinse the cut potatoes in water then dry them thoroughly with paper towel.

2. Cut each garlic clove in half lengthwise. Place the fries and the garlic into the ActiFry Pan and drizzle evenly with the oil. Cook for 30-35 minutes or until the fries are crisp and the garlic is deep golden brown. Season with salt.

Nutrients / serving ———— **200** calories

[3.5 g total fat ~ 0 g saturated fat ~ 2 g monounsaturated fat ~ 1 g polyunsaturated fat
0 mg cholesterol ~ 40 g carbohydrates ~ 6 g fiber ~ 3 g protein ~ 110 mg sodium]

✛ Nutritious

Excellent source of: Fiber, Vitamin
A, Vitamin B6, Manganese.
Good source of: Thiamin,
Pantothenic Acid, Copper,
Magnesium, Molybdenum,
Potassium.

Sweet Potato Fries
by *Ellie Krieger*

SERVES 4 · PREPARATION 10 min · COOKING 40/45 min

1 ¾ lbs sweet potatoes
(3 medium), unpeeled

1  canola oil

Salt, to taste

1 Cut the sweet potatoes into ½ inch thick fries. Rinse them in cold water, drain well, then dry them thoroughly with paper towel.

2 Put the potatoes in the ActiFry pan, drizzle with oil and cook for 40-45 minutes until they are tender and somewhat crisped. Season with salt and serve.

Variation For spicy Sweet Potatoes, toss the potatoes with half of the oil. Then, sprinkle with 2 teaspoons of chili powder and 1/8 teaspoon of cayenne pepper and toss.

Because of their high moisture content sweet potato fries don't crisp up the same way regular fries do. But they are delicious in their own right, plain or spicy.

Nutrients / serving

[7 g total fat ~ 0 g saturated fat ~ 0 g trans fat ~ 0 mg cholesterol
39 g carbohydrates ~ 3 g fiber ~ 5 g protein ~ 251 mg sodium ~ 932 mg potassium]

+ Nutritious

Excellent source of: Vitamin C.

Potato Wedges
with Herbs and Spices

SERVES 4 · PREPARATION 15 min · COOKING 35/40 min

1 ¾ lbs	Yukon gold potatoes
½ 🥄	Italian seasoning
½ 🥄	paprika
2 🥄	vegetable oil, divided
½ tsp	each salt and pepper (approx.)

1. Halve the potatoes lengthwise and cut each half into long, thin wedges. Rinse wedges thoroughly in water; drain well. Use a clean kitchen towel to thoroughly dry the wedges.

2. Place the wedges in a large bowl. Toss gently with the seasoning, paprika and half of the oil to coat wedges evenly.

3. Transfer the wedges to the ActiFry pan. Drizzle with remaining oil. Cook for 35 to 40 minutes or until the wedges are crispy, golden and cooked through. Season wedges with salt and pepper (adjust to taste).

Variation Substitute any dried herb blend you prefer for the Italian seasoning.

If using baby new potatoes, cut the potatoes in half rather than into wedges and proceed with the recipe as directed above.

Cajun Spiced
Potato Wedges

SERVES 4 · PREPARATION 15 min · COOKING 35/40 min

1 ¾ lbs	Yukon gold potatoes
½ 	Cajun seasoning
2	vegetable oil, divided
½ tsp	each salt and pepper (approx.)
	Chopped fresh parsley leaves (optional)

1 Halve the potatoes lengthwise and cut each half into long, thin wedges. Rinse wedges thoroughly in water. Use a clean kitchen towel to thoroughly dry the wedges.

2 Place the wedges in a large bowl. Toss gently with seasoning and half of the oil to coat wedges evenly.

3 Transfer the wedges to the ActiFry pan. Drizzle with the remaining oil. Cook for 35 to 40 minutes or until the wedges are crisp, golden and cooked through.

4 Season with salt and pepper (adjust to taste); garnish with chopped fresh parsley (if using).

Variation Substitute Garlic & Herb, Jamaican Jerk or Barbecue seasoning for the Cajun seasoning called for above.

Nutrients / serving —— **120** calories

[3.5 g total fat ~ 0 g saturated fat ~ 2 g monoinsatured fat ~ 1 g polyinsatured fat
0 mg cholesterol ~ 21 g carbohydrates ~ 3 g fiber ~ 3 g protein ~ 300 mg sodium]

⊕ Nutritious

Excellent source of: Vitamin C.
Good source of: Fiber, Vitamin
B6, Vitamin K, Manganese,
Potassium.

Home Fries by Ellie Krieger

SERVES 4 · PREPARATION 10 min · COOKING 50 min

1	medium onion, cut into ½ inch pieces
½	medium green pepper, cut into ½ inch pieces
1	canola oil, divided
1 lb	new red potatoes, unpeeled
½ tsp	salt, plus more to taste
¼ tsp	freshly ground black pepper, plus more to taste

1. Put the onion and pepper into the ActiFry Pan. Drizzle with ½ ActiFry spoon of oil, and cook for 15 minutes.

2. In the meantime, cut the potatoes into 1 inch chunks. Rinse them under water then dry them well with paper towel.

3. Transfer the cooked onions and peppers to a bowl. Put the potatoes into the ActiFry pan, drizzle with the remaining ½ spoonful of oil and cook for 30 minutes. Add the onions and peppers back to the pan and cook for 5 minutes more. Season with salt and pepper.

Nutrients / serving —

[8 g total fat ~ 1 g saturated fat ~ 0 g trans fat ~ 0 mg cholesterol
40 g carbohydrates ~ 3 g fiber ~ 5 g protein ~ 248 mg sodium ~ 933 mg potassium]

✦ Nutritious

Excellent source of: Vitamin C.

Almond Crunch Fries

SERVES 4 · PREPARATION 15 min · COOKING 40 min

1 ¾ lbs	baking potatoes such as Yukon gold
2	ground almonds
2	peanut oil
½ tsp	salt (approx.)

1 Scrub the potatoes and cut (unpeeled) fries of equal thickness, each about ½ inch square thickness. Rinse fries thoroughly in water; drain well. Use a clean kitchen towel to thoroughly dry the fries.

2 Place the fries in a bowl. Toss gently with the ground almonds and oil to coat fries evenly.

3 Transfer the fries to the ActiFry pan. Cook for 40 minutes or until the fries are crisp, golden and cooked through.

4 Season fries with salt (adjust to taste).

Variations Choose ground hazelnuts or peanuts instead of almonds.

— **245** calories

Ground nuts are available in the baking section of the supermarket.
Or, use a food processor to grind whole almonds finely.

Sauces
and Dips

38 calories ——— Nutrients / serving
(2 tbsp)

[3 g total fat ~ 1 g saturated fat ~ 0 g trans fat ~ 5 mg cholesterol ~ 2 g carbohydrates
0 g fiber ~ 0 g protein ~ 107 mg sodium ~ 22 mg potassium]

Creamy
Cocktail Dip

MAKES **1 ½ cups** · PREPARATION **5** min

½ cup	light mayonnaise
¼ cup	light sour cream
2	ketchup (approx.)
1 tsp	each lemon juice and prepared horseradish
½ tsp	Worcestershire sauce
	Dash hot pepper sauce (optional)
	Salt and pepper (optional)

1 Stir the mayonnaise with the sour cream until well combined. Add the ketchup, lemon juice, horseradish and Worcestershire sauce; stir until well combined.

2 Season to taste with hot pepper sauce, salt and pepper (if using). For an attractive garnish, top with an additional drop of ketchup; pull the tip of a knife through the dot to make a swirl shape.

Nutrients / serving —— **50 calories**
(2 tbsp)
[4 g total fat ~ 2 g saturated fat ~ 0 g trans fat ~ 12 mg cholesterol ~ 2 g carbohydrates
0 g fiber ~ 2 g protein ~ 44 mg sodium ~ 75 mg potassium]

Savory Garlic
and Chive Dip

MAKES **1 cup** · PREPARATION **5** min

1 cup	light sour cream
2	grated Parmesan cheese
1	green onion, finely chopped
1	snipped fresh chives (approx.)
½ tsp	minced garlic
	Salt and pepper (optional)

1 Stir the sour cream with the Parmesan cheese, green onion, chives and garlic until combined.

2 Season to taste with salt and pepper (if using). Garnish with additional chives.

Variation — Stir in 1 tsp finely grated lemon zest to add a fresh, bright flavor.

37 calories ——— Nutrients / serving
(2 tbsp)

[3 g total fat ~ 1 g saturated fat ~ 0 g trans fat ~ 3 mg cholesterol
2 g carbohydrates ~ 1 g fiber ~ 1 g protein ~ 10 mg sodium ~ 108 mg potassium]

Avocado Dip

MAKES **1 ¾ cups** · PREPARATION **10** min

1	avocado, peeled and pitted
1	tomato, seeded and chopped
½ cup	light sour cream
2	chopped green onion or chopped fresh coriander leaves
1	lime or lemon juice
1	clove garlic, minced
	Dash hot pepper sauce
	Salt and pepper (optional)

1 Combine the avocado, tomato, sour cream, green onion, lime juice, garlic and hot pepper sauce in a food processor. Pulse until well combined but still slightly chunky.

2 Season to taste with salt and pepper (if using).

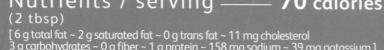

Nutrients / serving —— **70** calories
(2 tbsp)
[6 g total fat ~ 2 g saturated fat ~ 0 g trans fat ~ 11 mg cholesterol
3 g carbohydrates ~ 0 g fiber ~ 1 g protein ~ 158 mg sodium ~ 39 mg potassium]

Roasted Red Pepper Dip

MAKES **1 cup** · PREPARATION **5** min

½ cup	light sour cream
½ cup	light mayonnaise
⅓ cup	chopped roasted red peppers
2	chopped fresh basil leaves (approx.)
1	small clove garlic, minced
	Salt and pepper (optional)

1 Combine the sour cream, mayonnaise, red peppers, basil and garlic in a blender or food processor. Pulse until well combined and smooth.

2 Season to taste with salt and pepper (if using). Garnish with additional whole or chopped fresh basil leaves.

52 calories ——— Nutrients / serving
(2 tbsp)
[4 g total fat ~ 2 g saturated fat ~ 0 g trans fat ~ 12 mg cholesterol
2 g carbohydrates ~ 0 g fiber ~ 2 g protein ~ 118 mg sodium ~ 53 mg potassium]

Blue Cheese Dip

MAKES **1 ½ cups** · PREPARATION **20** min

½ cup	crumbled Roquefort cheese
1 cup	light sour cream
2	finely chopped red onion
1	snipped fresh chives
1 tsp	each granulated sugar and red wine vinegar
	Salt and pepper (optional)

1 Mash the cheese with half the sour cream until well combined. Stir in the remaining sour cream, red onion, chives, sugar and vinegar until well combined.

2 Season to taste with salt and pepper (if using). Let the dip stand for 15 minutes before serving.

Variation   Substitute other blue cheeses such as Stilton or Gorgonzola for the Roquefort.

Nutrients / serving —— **23 calories**

(2 tbsp)

[1 g total fat ~ 0 g saturated fat ~ 0 g trans fat ~ 1 mg cholesterol ~ 3 g carbohydrates
0 g fiber ~ 1 g protein ~ 17 mg sodium ~ 97 mg potassium]

Sweet Curry Dip

MAKES **1 cup** · PREPARATION **20** min

1 cup	thick yogurt
2	mango chutney (approx.)
2	chopped fresh cilantro or green onion
½	curry paste or powder
½ tsp	ground cumin
	Salt and pepper (optional)

1 Stir the yogurt with the mango chutney, cilantro or green onion, curry paste and cumin until well combined.

2 Season to taste with salt and pepper (if using). Let the dip stand for 15 minutes before serving. Garnish with additional mango chutney.

Gourmet Poultry
and Meat Recipes

Nutrients / serving

[9 g total fat ~ 1 g saturated fat ~ 0 g trans fat ~ 78 mg cholesterol ~ 26 g carbohydrates
1 g fiber ~ 31 g protein ~ 594 mg sodium ~ 543 mg potassium]

Saucy Chicken
with Pineapple

+ Nutritious

For additional color and to provide beneficial nutrients such as vitamins A and C, add chopped fresh red and orange peppers along with the pineapple mixture.
Excellent source of: Niacin, Vitamin B6.

SERVES **4** · PREPARATION **15** min · COOKING **15** min

1 lb	boneless, skinless chicken breast, sliced into thin strips
2	cornstarch, divided
½ tsp	each salt and pepper
2	vegetable oil
1 can	pineapple chunks, drained (juice reserved)
½	ground ginger
½	mild curry powder
2	reduced-sodium soy sauce
1 cup	cold water
1	lightly packed brown sugar
2	reserved pineapple juice

1 Toss the chicken strips with half of the cornstarch, salt and pepper. Transfer the chicken to the ActiFry pan. Drizzle evenly with the oil. Cook for 5 minutes.

2 Stir pineapple chunks with the ginger, curry powder, soy sauce and remaining salt and pepper until combined. Add pineapple mixture to the ActiFry pan. Let stand, covered, in the ActiFry for 5 minutes to marinate.

3 Whisk the water, remaining cornstarch, brown sugar and reserved pineapple juice until combined. Add to the ActiFry pan. Cook for 10 minutes or until chicken is tender and cooked through.

Serve over hot,
cooked basmati rice
or rice noodles.

260 calories —— Nutrients / serving

[13 g total fat ~ 4.5 g saturated fat ~ 5 g monoinsatured fat ~ 2.75 g polyinsatured fat
65 mg cholesterol ~ 9 g carbohydrates ~ 2 g fiber ~ 25 g protein ~ 390 mg sodium]

✚ Nutritious

Excellent source of: Protein,
Vitamin A, Niacin, Vitamin B6,
Vitamin C, Vitamin K, Iron,
Phosphorus, Selenium.
Good source of: Riboflavin,
Manganese, Molybdenum,
Potassium.

Spicy Thai
Chicken Curry

SERVES **4** · PREPARATION **15** min · COOKING **18** min

1 lb	boneless, skinless chicken breast, sliced into thin strips
1 tsp	minced fresh gingerroot
½ tsp	each salt and pepper
1	clove garlic, minced
1	small red chili pepper, seeded and chopped
2	canola oil, divided
1	each red and green pepper, thinly sliced
1	medium zucchini, sliced
1 cup	lite coconut milk
2 tsp	cornstarch
1 tsp	green Thai curry paste
2	chopped fresh coriander
	Lime wedges (optional)

1 Place the chicken strips, gingerroot, salt, pepper, chili pepper and garlic in the ActiFry pan. Drizzle evenly with half of the oil. Cook for 8 minutes or until browned. Transfer the chicken to a bowl; reserve. Add the peppers, zucchini and remaining oil to the ActiFry pan. Cook for 5 minutes.

2 Meanwhile, whisk the lite coconut milk with the cornstarch and curry paste until smooth. Add this mixture and the reserved chicken to the ActiFry pan. Cook for 5 minutes or until sauce is thickened and chicken is cooked through.

3 Stir in the coriander. Serve with lime wedges (if using).

Variation Substitute turkey breast for the chicken.

Serve the curry over steamed rice or warm rice noodles.

Nutrients / serving —— **600** calories

(including rice)

[19 g total fat ~ 5 g saturated fat ~ 8 g monoinsaturated fat ~ 3.5 g polyinsatured fat
90 mg cholesterol ~ 72 g carbohydrates ~ 4 g fiber ~ 32 g protein ~ 580 mg sodium]

✚ Nutritious

Excellent source of: Protein, Vitamin A, Thiamin, Riboflavin, Niacin, Vitamin B6, Vitamin C, Folate, Vitamin K, Iron, Manganese, Phosphorus, Potassium, Selenium, Zinc.
Good source of: Fiber, Pantothenic Acid, Calcium, Copper, Magnesium.

Chicken Gumbo by *Ellie Krieger*

SERVES **4** • PREPARATION **20** min • COOKING **40-47** min

1 lb	skinless boneless chicken thigh, cut into 1-inch cubes
½	olive oil
1	small onion, chopped
1	medium green pepper, diced
1 cup	cup fresh okra, trimmed and sliced into ¼-inch pieces (about 3 ½ oz.)
1	link (about 3 oz.) pre-cooked Andouille sausage, diced
2	stalks celery, chopped
3	cloves garlic, minced
1	bay leaf
½ tsp	salt
½ tsp	paprika
¼ tsp	cayenne pepper
¼ cup	all purpose flour
1 ½ cups	low-sodium chicken broth
1 14.5 oz.	can low-sodium stewed tomatoes, including juice

1 Place the chicken in the ActiFry pan, drizzle it with the oil and cook until chicken is just cooked through, 10 minutes. Transfer the chicken to a plate, leaving the drippings in pan.

2 Add the onion, pepper, okra, sausage, celery, garlic, bay leaf, salt, paprika and cayenne to the ActiFry pan and cook until the onions are tender and the okra is tender but firm, about 20 minutes.

3 In a small bowl, whisk the flour with ½ cup of the chicken broth until dissolved. Add the dissolved flour with ½ cup of stock, and tomatoes with juice to pan. Return chicken to pan and cook for 10 minutes, or until mixture has thickened When most of the stock has evaporated, add another ½ cup of stock and cook 5 minutes more. Serve over rice, garnished with parsley with hot sauce on the side.

For serving
4 cups cooked rice
2 tablespoons chopped fresh parsley leaves Hot pepper sauce, to taste.

Serve with steamed rice, boiled potatoes or egg noodles and steamed green beans or broccoli.

— Nutrients / serving

[9 g total fat ~ 2 g saturated fat ~ 0 g trans fat ~ 33 mg cholesterol ~ 9 g carbohydrates
1 g fiber ~ 27 g protein ~ 66 mg sodium ~ 535 mg potassium]

➕ Nutritious

Excellent source of: Vitamin C,
Niacin, Vitamin B6.

Turkey
with 3 Peppers

· SERVES **4** · PREPARATION **15** min · COOKING **20/25** min

1	each red, green and yellow pepper, thinly sliced
2	olive oil
2	cloves garlic, minced
1	red onion, thinly sliced
4	port or cooking sherry
½	cider vinegar
1 tsp	cornstarch
1 lb	boneless, skinless turkey breast, sliced into thin strips
	Salt and pepper (optional)

1 Place the peppers in the ActiFry pan. Drizzle evenly with the oil. Cook for 5 minutes. Add the garlic and onion to the ActiFry pan. Cook for 5 minutes.

2 Whisk the port with the vinegar and cornstarch until combined. Add the turkey breast strips and the port mixture to the ActiFry pan. Cook for 10 to 15 minutes or until the turkey is tender and cooked through. Season to taste with salt and pepper (if using).

Variation Substitute boneless chicken breast or pork tenderloin for the turkey.

49

310 calories ———— Nutrients / serving

[9 g total fat ~ 2 g saturated fat ~ 2 g monoinsatured fat ~ 0.5 g polyinsatured fat
40 mg cholesterol ~ 34 g carbohydrates ~ 11 g fiber ~ 23 g protein ~ 570 mg sodium]

➕ Nutritious

Excellent source of: Protein, Fiber, Vitamin A, Thiamin, Vitamin K, Magnesium, Phosphorus, Potassium, Zinc. Good source of: Riboflavin, Folate, Calcium, Iodine, Iron, Manganese.

Tuscan white beans
with sausage by *Ellie Krieger*

SERVES **4** · PREPARATION **10** min · COOKING **30** min

½	olive oil
2	links (6 ounces) precooked Italian style chicken sausage, diced
1	small onion, diced
3	cloves garlic, sliced
2 15.5 oz	cans canellini beans, preferably low-sodium, drained and rinsed
1 cup	low-sodium chicken broth
4 cups	escarole (3 oz.), coarsely chopped
2 tsp	chopped fresh sage
¼ tsp	salt
½ tsp	chili flakes
¼ cup	freshly grated Parmesan cheese

1 Place the oil and sausage in the ActiFry pan. Cook for 8 minutes, until sausage is browned on all sides. Add the onions and garlic and cook until onions are tender, another 8 minutes.

2 Add the beans, broth, escarole, sage, salt and chili flakes. Cook an additional 15 minutes, until mixture has thickened. Divide among 4 bowls and garnish each with 1 tablespoon of cheese.

Nutrients / serving —— 356 calories

[11 g total fat ~ 3 g saturated fat ~ 0 g trans fat ~ 97 mg cholesterol ~ 28 g carbohydrates
2 g fiber ~ 35 g protein ~ 479 mg sodium ~ 888 mg potassium]

✚ Nutritious

Excellent source of: Niacin, Riboflavin, Thiamine, Vitamin B6, Vitamin B12, Zinc.

Sweet and Sour
Pork Tenderloin

SERVES **4** · PREPARATION **15** min · COOKING **20** min

1		olive oil
2		onions, thinly sliced
1 ¼ lb		pork tenderloin, cut into thin strips
1 ½		cornstarch (approx.), divided
2		cloves garlic, minced
1 ¼ cups		plain tomato sauce
⅔ cup		apple juice
4		red wine
2		brown sugar
2		red wine vinegar
1		tomato paste

1 Place the onions and oil in the ActiFry pan. Cook for 5 minutes. Meanwhile, toss the pork with ½ ActiFry spoon cornstarch and garlic. Reserve. Whisk the remaining cornstarch with the tomato sauce; stir in the apple juice, red wine, brown sugar, red wine vinegar and tomato paste until combined. Reserve.

2 Add the pork mixture to the ActiFry pan. Cook for 5 minutes. (If necessary, stir the pork with a wooden spoon if necessary to separate the strips.)

3 Add the tomato sauce mixture to the ActiFry pan. Cook for 10 minutes or until the pork is tender and the sauce is thickened.

Variation

Substitute lean beef, lamb or chicken breast for the pork.

Serve with steamed rice, buttered egg noodles or mashed potatoes.

51

Nutrients / serving

[11 g total fat ~ 2.5 g saturated fat ~ 2 g monoinsatured fat ~ 4 g polyinsatured fat
50 mg cholesterol ~ 16 g carbohydrates ~ 30 g protein ~ 390 mg sodium]

+ Nutritious

Excellent source of: Protein, Vitamin A, Niacin, Vitamin B12, Vitamin C, Folate, Zinc Good source of: Fiber, Vitamin B6, Iron, Manganese, Potassium.

Sesame beef
with broccoli
by Ellie Krieger

SERVES **4** • PREPARATION **15** min • COOKING **20-25** min

1 lb	top round, London broil or flank steak, thinly sliced
½	canola oil
1	small onion, thinly sliced
1	red bell pepper, seeded and thinly sliced
3	cloves garlic, thinly sliced
2 tsp	minced fresh ginger
¾ cup	low sodium beef broth
3	low-sodium soy sauce
1	sesame oil
1	tablespoon honey
2 tsp	cornstarch dissolved in 2 tablespoons cold water
¼ tsp	chili flakes
5 cups	broccoli florets (about 8 oz. florets)
4 tsp	toasted sesame seeds

1   Place the beef in the ActiFry pan, drizzle with the canola oil and cook until meat is browned on all sides and just cooked, 8 minutes. Transfer the meat to a plate.

2   Add the onion and pepper to the ActiFry pan and cook until tender, 9 to 10 minutes.

3   Add the garlic and ginger and cook an additional 3 minutes.

4   In a small bowl whisk together the beef broth, soy sauce, sesame oil, honey, cornstarch and chili flakes and add to pan with beef.
Stir in broccoli, and cook an additional 5 minutes, until broccoli is just tender and liquid as thickened slightly.

5   Divide among 4 plates and sprinkle with sesame seeds.

— **260** calories

✚ Nutritious

To reduce the fat, substitute lean turkey meatballs for the regular beef meatballs.
Excellent source of: Vitamin C.

For a crowd-pleasing appetizer, omit the peppers and serve the saucy meatballs with toothpicks.

— Nutrients / serving
(1/6th portion)

[13 g total fat ~ 5 g saturated fat ~ 0 g trans fat ~ 49 mg cholesterol
15 g carbohydrates ~ 2 g fiber ~ 14 g protein ~ 770 mg sodium ~ 424 mg potassium]

Sweet and Saucy
Meatballs

SERVES **4/6** · PREPARATION **10** min · COOKING **20** min

1 lb	frozen beef meatballs
1	each red and yellow pepper, cubed
¾ cup	apple or pineapple juice (approx.)
4 🥄	ketchup
1 🥄	each prepared mustard and maple syrup or brown sugar
1 🥄	each cider vinegar and grated onion
1 tsp	each minced garlic
1 tsp	cornstarch
	Chopped fresh coriander leaves (optional)
	Hot, cooked white or brown rice (optional)

1 Place the meatballs and peppers in the ActiFry pan.

2 Whisk apple juice with the ketchup, mustard, maple syrup, cider vinegar, onion, garlic and cornstarch. Add to the ActiFry pan.

3 Cook for 20 minutes or until meatballs are cooked through and sauce is thickened. (Add a couple extra spoonfuls of juice if the sauce becomes too thick.) Sprinkle with coriander (if using); serve over rice (if using).

Variation
For a tropical version, stir in 1 cup drained pineapple chunks when adding the peppers.

55

Nutrients / serving

[9 g total fat ~ 2 g saturated fat ~ 4.7 g monoinsatured fat ~ 1 g polyinsatured fat
60 mg cholesterol ~ 35 g carbohydrates ~ 9 g fiber ~ 32 g protein ~ 830 mg sodium]

Chipotle Beef Chili by *Ellie Krieger*

SERVES 4 · PREPARATION 5 min · COOKING 45 min

1	small onion, chopped
1	medium red pepper, chopped
1 	olive oil
1 lb	of lean ground beef
2 tsp	ground cumin
1 tsp	ground coriander
1 15.5 oz.	can of fire-roasted crushed tomatoes
½ cup	water
1	canned chipotle chili in adobo sauce, seeded and minced (about 2 tsp), plus 1 tsp of the sauce
½ tsp	dried oregano
1 15.5 oz	can of black beans, preferably low sodium
	Salt and freshly ground pepper, to taste

1 Place the onion and pepper in the ActiFry pan, drizzle with oil and cook for 6 minutes. Crumble the beef into the ActiFry pan. Add the cumin and coriander and cook for 5 minutes, until the meat is browned.

2 Break up any large pieces of browned meat with a wooden spoon. Add the tomatoes, ¼ cup of the water, chipotle with adobo sauce, and oregano and cook for 25 minutes.

3 Add the beans and the remaining ¼ cup of water and cook for 10 minutes more. Season with salt and pepper to taste.

— **330 calories**

➕ Nutritious

Excellent source of: Protein, Fiber, Vitamin A, Niacin, Vitamin B12, Vitamin C, Iron, Zinc.
Good source of: Magnesium, Potassium.

Gourmet
Seafood Recipes

335 calories — Nutrients / serving

[17 g total fat ~ 1 g saturated fat ~ 0 g trans fat ~ 95 mg cholesterol
29 g carbohydrates ~ 7 g fiber ~ 20 g protein ~ 2507 mg sodium ~ 1018 mg potassium]

✚ Nutritious

Excellent source of: Folate, Vitamin C, Vitamin A, Vitamin B6, Vitamin B12, Iron.

Crunchy Green Vegetable Stir-Fry with Shrimp

SERVES 2 • PREPARATION 5 min • COOKING 13 min

1	onion, thinly sliced
1	clove garlic, finely chopped
1	hot chili pepper, seeded and sliced (optional)
2	vegetable oil
2	small zucchinis sliced on an angle
1 ½ cups	sugar snap peas or snow peas
⅓ cup	cold water
4 oz	jumbo shrimp, peeled, de-veined with tails on
3	green onions thinly sliced
4	Asian black bean sauce
1	chopped cilantro (approx.)

1. Place the onion, garlic and chili pepper (if using) in the ActiFry pan. Drizzle evenly with the oil. Cook for 5 minutes.

2. Add the zucchini, snap peas and water to the ActiFry pan; cook for 5 minutes or until the vegetables are tender-crisp.

3. Add the shrimp, green onions, black bean sauce and cilantro to the ActiFry pan. Cook for 3 minutes or until shrimp is opaque. Sprinkle with additional cilantro to garnish.

Variation Substitute bean sprouts for the snap peas.

Serve with hot, cooked rice.

60

Nutrients / serving —— **217** calories

[7 g total fat ~ 1 g saturated fat ~ 0 g trans fat ~ 21 mg cholesterol
23 g carbohydrates ~ 2 g fiber ~ 7 g protein ~ 41 mg sodium ~ 618 mg potassium]

✛ Nutritious

Excellent source of: Vitamin C.

Baby New Potatoes
with Garlic, Tomato and Shrimp

SERVES 4 · PREPARATION 10 min · COOKING 31 min

1 lb	baby new potatoes, halved
8	cloves garlic, peeled
2 🥄	olive oil, divided
2	plum tomatoes, seeded and chopped
12	jumbo shrimp, peeled, de-veined with tails on
1 🥄	chopped fresh tarragon or parsley leaves
	Salt and pepper (optional)

1 Place the potatoes and garlic in the ActiFry pan. Drizzle evenly with half the olive oil. Cook for 25 minutes or until potatoes are fork tender.

2 Remove the garlic and mash it with the remaining oil to make a paste. Add the garlic paste, tomatoes and shrimp to the ActiFry pan. Cook for 6 minutes or until shrimp is opaque.

3 Season to taste with salt and pepper (if using); stir in the tarragon or parsley.

Serve with a tossed green salad.

— Nutrients / serving

[8 g total fat ~ 1.1 g saturated fat ~ 5 g monoinsatured fat ~ 1.1 g polyinsatured fat
45 mg cholesterol ~ 10 g carbohydrates ~ 3 g fiber ~ 27 g protein ~ 520 mg sodium]

Nutritious

Excellent source of: Folate, Magnesium, Phosphorus, Potassium, Protein, Selenium Vitamin A, Vitamin C, Vitamin K
Good source of: Copper, Fiber, Iron, Manganese, Zinc.

Scallops and Asparagus Sauté with Lemon and Thyme by Ellie Krieger

SERVES **4** · PREPARATION **10** min · COOKING **12** min

1 ¼ lbs	bay scallops
1	bunch of asparagus (about 1 pound)
¼ cup	diced shallot
2	olive oil
1	fresh chopped thyme leaves
2 tsp	finely grated lemon zest
½ tsp	salt
¼ tsp	freshly ground black pepper
2	fresh lemon juice

1 Rinse the scallops and pat dry with paper towel. Trim the asparagus and cut on the bias into 1 inch pieces.

2 Place the shallots into the ActiFry pan, drizzle with ½ spoonful of oil and cook for 3 minutes. Add the thyme, lemon zest, asparagus, scallops salt and pepper.

3 Drizzle with the remaining oil and cook for 9 minutes, until the scallops are opaque and the asparagus is crisp-tender. Drizzle with the lemon juice.

4 Serve with the accumulated juices, over rice.

63

Nutrients / serving

[8 g total fat ~ 2.8 g saturated fat ~ 2.6 g monoinsatured fat ~ 2.3 g polyinsatured fat
60 mg cholesterol ~ 7 g carbohydrates ~ 1 g fiber ~ 21 g protein ~ 80 mg sodium]

Salmon Tandoori
with Yogurt Sauce

SERVES 4 • PREPARATION 20 min • COOKING 5 min

12	cubes of 1 oz of fresh salmon
1½ 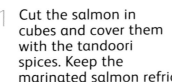	of tandoori spices
3	yogurt (1½ cups)
½	cucumber, seeded
4 g	of green chilli pepper
½	red onion
1	small tomato, seeded
½ tsp	of cumin (powder)
30	fresh mint leaves

1 Cut the salmon in cubes and cover them with the tandoori spices. Keep the marinated salmon refrigerated.

2 Mix ¼ of the yogurt with the green chilli, mint, cumin, salt and pepper. Keep the mix refrigerated.

3 Peel the tomato, take out the seeds and cut into small cubes. Peel and slice the onion very thin. Peel the cucumber and cut in cubes.

4 Put the seasoned salmon in the ActiFry for 5 to 6 min. In the mean time, add to the yogurt mix, the rest of yogurt, the tomato cubes, the cucumber cubes, and the onion slices. Serve the salmon cubes with the sauce in small bowls. When you cook the salmon for 5 to 6 min, the salmon is still half-cooked. If you wish to have it well done, add 4 to 5 min to the initial cooking time.

✛ Nutritious

This fresh recipe with oriental flavors is rich in essential nutrients. Salmon is one of the richest foods in omega 3 fatty acids which can benefit the cardiovascular system. This recipe also provides fiber from cucumber and calcium from yogurt.
Excellent source of: Molybdenum, Phosphorus, Protein, Selenium
Good source of: Calcium, Copper, Iodine, Magnesium, Pantothenic Acid, Potassium, Vitamin C.

Gourmet
Vegetable Recipes

283 calories ———— Nutrients / serving

[8 g total fat ~ 1 g saturated fat ~ 0 g trans fat ~ 0 mg cholesterol
47 g carbohydrates ~ 10 g fiber ~ 10 g protein ~ 310 mg sodium ~ 318 mg potassium]

✚ **Nutritious**

Excellent source of: Vitamin C.

Mixed Vegetable Medley

SERVES 4 · PREPARATION 15 min · COOKING 25 min

1	red pepper, thinly sliced
1	red onion, thinly sliced
1 🥄	vegetable oil
2 cups	thawed, frozen baby corn cobs
1 cup	julienned or thinly sliced carrots
1 cup	sliced mixed mushrooms
1	can (8 oz) sliced bamboo shoots, drained and rinsed
2	cloves garlic, minced
	Pinch ground cardamom
1 🥄	reduced-sodium soy sauce
	Dash hot sauce (optional)
1 cup	warm vegetable broth, divided
½ 🥄	cornstarch
	Thinly sliced green onion (optional)

1 Place the red pepper and onion in the ActiFry pan. Drizzle evenly with vegetable oil. Cook for 5 minutes.

2 Add the corn cobs, carrots, mushrooms, bamboo shoots, garlic, cardamom, soy sauce and hot sauce (if using) to the ActiFry pan. Pour in ⅔ cup of the broth. Cook for 15 minutes. (If necessary, open lid and stir with a wooden spoon to free the vegetables at the side of the pan.)

3 Whisk the remaining broth with the cornstarch to make a smooth paste. Stir into the vegetables. Cook for 5 minutes or until the sauce is slightly thickened. Garnish with green onions (if using).

Serve with steamed white or brown rice or cooked rice noodles.

Nutrients / serving —— 210 calories

[4 g total fat ~ 0.5 g saturated fat ~ 2.5 g monoinsaturated fat ~ 0.5 g polyinsatured fat
0 mg cholesterol ~ 42 g carbohydrates ~ 9 g fiber ~ 4 g protein ~ 370 mg sodium]

+ Nutritious

Excellent source of: Fiber, Vitamin A, Vitamin B6, Vitamin C, Folate, Vitamin K, Manganese, Potassium.
Good source of: Thiamin, Pantothenic Acid, Copper, Magnesium, Molybdenum, Phosphorus.

Balsamic glazed
root vegetables by Ellie Krieger

SERVES 4 · PREPARATION 15 min · COOKING 35/40 min

14	cloves garlic, peeled
1	red onion, cut into 8 wedges
2	parsnips cut into chunks (about 1 lb.)
1	medium sweet potato (skin-on), cut into ½-inch thick half-moons (about 9 ounces)
2	large carrots, cut into sticks
½ tsp	salt
¼ tsp	freshly ground black pepper
1 🥄	olive oil
1	sprig rosemary (about 6 inches)
3 🥄	balsamic vinegar

1 Place the garlic, onion, parsnips, sweet potato, carrot in the ActiFry pan.

2 Sprinkle with salt and pepper and drizzle with the oil. Cook for 15 minutes.

3 Add the rosemary to the pan and cook for 15 minutes more until the vegetables are softened and browned.

4 Add the balsamic vinegar and cook an additional 5-10 minutes.

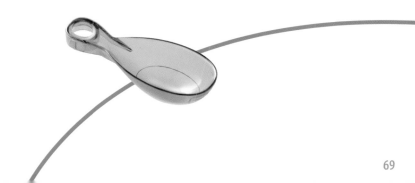

[5 g total fat ~ 0.5 g saturated fat ~ 3.5 g monounsaturated fat ~ 1 g polyunsaturated fat
0 mg cholesterol ~ 8 g carbohydrates ~ 4 g fiber ~ 3 g protein ~ 5 mg sodium]

✚ Nutritious

Excellent source of: Vitamin K.
Good source of: Fiber, Vitamin A,
Folate, Magnesium, Manganese.

Green Beans
with Almonds and Parsley *by Ellie Krieger*

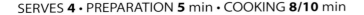

SERVES 4 • PREPARATION 5 min • COOKING 8/10 min

¾ lb	fresh green beans
½ cup	slivered almonds (not sliced)
½ 🥄	olive oil
¼ tsp	finely grated lemon zest
1 🥄	fresh lemon juice
¼ cup	chopped fresh parsley leaves
	Salt and freshly ground black pepper, to taste

1 Wash and trim the green beans and cut them on the bias into 1 inch pieces. Put the almonds into the ActiFry pan and cook for 3 minutes. Add the green beans to the pan and drizzle with the oil.

2 Cook for an additional 7 minutes, until the beans are crisp-tender.

3 Transfer the green beans and almonds to a serving bowl. Add the lemon zest, lemon juice, and parsley and stir to combine. Season with salt and pepper. Serve warm or at room temperature.

79 calories ——— Nutrients / serving
(⅛th recipe or ½ cup)
[4 g total fat ~ 1 g saturated fat ~ 0 g trans fat ~ 0 mg cholesterol ~ 8 g carbohydrates
1 g fiber ~ 1 g protein ~ 578 mg sodium ~ 353 mg potassium]

 **Nutritious**

This light low fat sauce will go best with starchy food and mixed fried vegetables.

Tomato and Basil Pasta Sauce

SERVES 4 · PREPARATION 20 min · COOKING 30 min

1	small onion, chopped
2	cloves garlic, minced
½ tsp	dried thyme leaves
½ tsp	each salt and pepper (approx.)
2	olive oil
2	cans (28 oz) diced tomatoes, drained
⅓ cup	dry red wine
1	tomato paste
3	chopped fresh basil
½ tsp	granulated sugar (approx.)

1 Place the onion, garlic, thyme, salt and pepper to the ActiFry pan. Drizzle evenly with the oil. Cook for 8 minutes.

2 Add the tomatoes, red wine and tomato paste. Cook for 30 minutes or until sauce is thickened.

3 Stir in the basil and sugar. Taste and adjust salt, pepper and sugar as needed.

Variations

Customize this recipe by adding seasonings such as dried oregano leaves, hot pepper flakes and fennel seed when adding the dried thyme.

Reserve some of the canned tomato juices so that you can adjust the consistency of the sauce if necessary.

Nutrients / serving ——— 190 calories

[7 g total fat ~ 2 g saturated fat ~ 3.5 g monounsaturated fat~ 7 g polyunsaturated fat
5 mg cholesterol ~ 26 g carbohydrates ~ 2 g fiber ~ 9 g protein ~ 310 mg sodium]

Nutritious

Excellent source of: Vitamin A.
Good source of: Phosphorus,
Protein.

Butternut
squash risotto by Ellie Krieger

SERVES **4** (side dish) • PREPARATION **10** min • COOKING **36** min

3 cups	low-sodium chicken broth
1	spoon olive oil
1	small onion, finely diced
½	cup Arborio rice
½	cup pureed butternut squash (½ of a 10 oz. package of frozen butternut squash puree, thawed)
¼	teaspoon salt
	pinch ground nutmeg
⅓ cup	freshly grated Parmesan cheese (1 ounce)

1 Heat the chicken broth in a pan on the stove until it is hot but not boiling.

2 Place the oil and onion in the ActiFry pan and cook until the onions are translucent, about 6 minutes.

3 Add the rice and 1 ½ cups of hot chicken broth and cook until the water is mostly absorbed and the rice is partially cooked, 15 minutes.

4 Add ½ cup of broth, squash, salt and nutmeg cook for 5 minutes.

5 Add another ½ cup of broth and cook for 5 minutes more.

6 Add the remaining ½ cup of broth and cook for 5 minutes more, until liquid is thickened and mostly absorbed.

7 Stir in all but 1 tablespoon of the cheese and cook an additional 2 minutes. Garnish with the remaining Parmesan cheese right before serving.

171 calories

Serve the curry with warm whole-wheat pitas, naan or cooked brown basmati rice. Serve yogurt and mango chutney on the side.

— Nutrients / serving

[11 g total fat ~ 1 g saturated fat ~ 0 g trans fat ~ 0 mg cholesterol
8 g carbohydrates ~ 1 g fiber ~ 11 g protein ~ 152 mg sodium ~ 68 mg potassium]

Excellent source of: Niacin, Vitamin C, Vitamin B6, Iron

Golden Tofu Curry

SERVES 4 · PREPARATION 10 min · COOKING 12 min

1 olive oil

1 mild Indian-style curry paste

½ cup each chopped onion and red pepper

1 clove garlic, minced

½ minced fresh ginger

1 lb firm or extra firm tofu, cubed

½ cup each frozen peas and vegetable broth

2 raisins

2 chopped fresh coriander

1 Stir the olive oil with the curry paste. Add the oil mixture, onion, red pepper, garlic and ginger to the ActiFry pan. Cook for 3 minutes.

2 Add the tofu to the ActiFry pan. Cook for 5 minutes.

3 Add the peas, broth and raisins. Cook for 4 minutes or until peas are vibrant green and tender. Sprinkle with coriander.

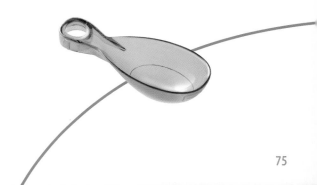

Gourmet
Dessert Recipes

Nutrients / serving —

[0 g total fat ~ 0 g saturated fat ~ 0 g trans fat ~ 0 mg cholesterol ~ 37 g carbohydrates
3 g fiber ~ 1 g protein ~ 2 mg sodium ~ 265 mg potassium]

✛ Nutritious

Excellent source of: Vitamin C.

Roasted Pineapple
with Figs and Honey

SERVES 4 · PREPARATION 5 min · COOKING 15 min

1	fresh, ripe pineapple
3	honey, divided
4	fresh figs
1	lemon juice
½ tsp	ground cinnamon, ginger or cardamom

1 Cut the top and base from the pineapple. Holding upright, use a sharp knife to cut down the sides of the fruit, removing the peel. Quarter the pineapple lengthwise. Remove and discard the centre core from each quarter; slice crossways into ½ inch thick pieces.

2 Place the pineapple in the ActiFry pan. Drizzle with 2 ActiFry spoons of the honey and lemon juice. Cook for 10 minutes.

3 Quarter the figs. Add the figs and cinnamon to the ActiFry pan. Drizzle with the remaining honey. Cook for 5 minutes.

Variation   Substitute chopped dried figs if the fresh fruit is out of seasons.

141 calories

Serve over sponge
cake, frozen yogurt
or ice cream.

Nutrients / serving

(not including whipped cream)

[0 g total fat ~ 0 g saturated fat ~ 0 g monoinsatured fat ~ 0 g polyinsatured fat
0 mg cholesterol ~ 23 g carbohydrates ~ 3 g fiber ~ 1 g protein ~ 0 mg sodium]

✚ Nutritious

Excellent source of Vitamin C.
Good source of: Fiber.

Mixed Berry Compote by *Ellie Krieger*

SERVES 6 · PREPARATION 5 min · COOKING 20 min

2 12 oz.	bags unsweetened frozen mixed berries, thawed
OR	8 oz each (about 2 cups each) fresh blueberries, raspberries and sliced strawberries
3 🥄	sugar, plus more to taste
2 🥄	orange liqueur
2 🥄	lemon juice
1 🥄	cornstarch, dissolved in 3 tablespoons cold water

1 Put the berries, 3 tablespoons of sugar, orange liqueur, lemon juice and dissolved cornstarch into the ActiFry pan and cook until the liquid has thickened and the fruit has softened, 20 minutes.

2 Add more sugar to taste if necessary.

3 Allow to cool slightly before serving or serve at room temperature.

This compote is delicious on its own with some whipped cream as a garnish, but it is also a versatile topping, wonderful on ice cream, angel food cake, or on pancakes and waffles.

160 calories ——— Nutrients / serving

[4 g total fat ~ 0 g saturated fat ~ 0 g trans fat ~ 0 mg cholesterol
34 g carbohydrates ~ 3 g fiber ~ 1 g protein ~ 3 mg sodium ~ 339 mg potassium]

✦ Nutritious

Leave the skin on the apples
for additional fiber content.

Glazed Apple Wedges

SERVES **4** · PREPARATION **10** min · COOKING **20** min

4	Granny Smith apples
1 🥄	vegetable oil
½ cup	chopped, dried apricots
2 🥄	maple syrup or honey
1 tsp	ground cinnamon

1 Peel and core the apples; cut into wedges. Place the apple wedges in a bowl. Toss the apples with the oil to coat wedges evenly.

2 Place the apples in the ActiFry pan.
Cook for 10 minutes. Add the apricots, maple syrup and cinnamon. Cook for 8 to 10 minutes or until apples are tender and well-glazed.

Variations

Substitute dried cranberries or raisins for the apricots.

Serve the apples topped with frozen yogurt and crumbled granola.

Nutrients / serving —— 193 calories

[9.0 g total fat ~ 0.7 g saturated fat ~ 4.5 g monoinsaturated fat ~ 2.4 g polyinsatured fat
0 mg cholesterol ~ 25 g carbohydrates ~ 3 g fiber ~ 4.2 g protein ~ 34 mg sodium]

✚ Nutritious

Good source of Fiber.
Excellent source of Manganese.

Cherry-Pecan Granola by Ellie Krieger

SERVES **4** · PREPARATION **10** min · COOKING **8** min

2 cups	rolled oats
¾ cup	coarsely chopped, unsalted pecans
½ 	canola oil
⅓ cup	pure maple syrup
½ tsp	vanilla extract
¼ tsp	ground cinnamon
⅛ tsp	salt
⅓ cup	dried cherries

1 Put the oats, pecans, oil, maple syrup, vanilla, cinnamon and salt in a large mixing bowl and stir until evenly coated.

2 Put the oat mixture into the ActiFry pan and cook for 7 minutes, until the oats and nuts are well toasted. Add the cherries and cook for one minute more.

3 Remove the ActiFry pan from its base and allow the mixture to cool for 15 minutes. It will crisp further as it cools. Store in an airtight container in the refrigerator for up to 2 weeks.

You can make this granola with any combination of chopped nuts and dried fruits you like or happen to have on hand.
Granola is great with milk or yogurt for breakfast or as an energizing snack.

158 calories

Serve the fruit over creamy vanilla frozen yogurt or ice cream, angel food cake or with fresh cheese such as ricotta.

— Nutrients / serving

[0 g total fat ~ 0 g saturated fat ~ 0 g trans fat ~ 0 mg cholesterol ~ 0.2 lipid
26.1 g carbohydrates ~ 3 g fiber ~1.3 g protein ~ 10 mg sodium ~ 308 mg potassium]

✛ Nutritious

An inventive and delicious recipe to finish your meal with a dessert containing vitamin and antioxidant-rich red fruit.

Dried Fruit Topping

SERVES 6 · PREPARATION 35 min · COOKING 20 min

1 cup	halved, dried apricots
½ cup	dried cranberries or sour cherries
¼ cup	dried blueberries
1 cup	each ice wine or dessert wine and white cranberry or white grape juice
1 tsp	finely grated orange zest

1 Place the apricots, cranberries, blueberries, ice wine and juice in a non-reactive bowl. Soak for 30 minutes.

2 Transfer the fruit and all liquid to the ActiFry pan. Cook for 20 minutes or until fruit is plump and liquid is slightly thickened.

3 Stir in the orange zest. Serve warm or store in an airtight container in the refrigerator for up to 1 week.

Variations

For an alcohol-free version, replace the ice wine with 1 cup of white cranberry juice or white grape juice.

NUTRITIOUS & DELICIOUS™

The cooking times may vary depending on the ripeness, size, total volume and individual preferences. Use these times as a guideline only.

Potatoes

	PREPARATION	QUANTITY	OIL	COOKING TIME
Fresh French Fries*	½" x ½"	2.2 lbs	1 Tbsp.	45 - 50 min.
	⅓" x ⅓"	2.2 lbs	1 Tbsp.	40 - 45 min.
	standard	1.65 lbs	¾ Tbsp.	40 - 45 min.
	standard	1.1 lbs	½ Tbsp.	30 - 37 min.
Frozen French fries	standard	½ lbs	¼ Tbsp.	24 - 28 min.
	Steak fries	28 oz bag	None	32 - 37 min.
	Golden	28 oz bag	None	25 - 30 min.
	Shoestring	28 oz bag	None	27 - 30 min.
Potatoes (quartered)	Fresh	2.2 lbs	1 Tbsp.	45 - 50 min.
	Frozen	24 oz bag	None	28 - 33 min.
Diced Potato	Fresh	2.2 lbs	1 Tbsp.	47 - 50 min.
	Frozen	28 oz bag	None	30 - 45 min.

Meat & Poultry

	PREPARATION	QUANTITY	OIL	COOKING TIME
Beef	Fresh (Sirloin cut into 1/4 inch thick strips)	1.3 lbs	None	8 - 10 min.
Chili con Carne	Fresh (made from ground beef)	1.1 lbs	1 Tbsp.	30 - 40 min.
Chinese spring rolls	Fresh	6 to 8 small pieces	1 Tbsp.	10 - 12 min.
	Frozen	10 pieces (8 oz)	None	10 - 12 min.
Chicken breasts (boneless)	Fresh	6 pieces (about ¼ lb each)	None	10 - 15 min.
Chicken drumsticks	Fresh	4 to 6 pieces	None	30 - 32 min.
Chicken legs	Fresh	2 pieces	None	30 - 35 min.
Chicken nuggets	Fresh	1.75 lbs	None	20 - 25 min
	Frozen	21 oz bag	None	12 - 15 min.
	Frozen	12 pieces (6.7 oz)	None	25 - 30 min.
Lamb chops	Fresh (1x1 inch thick)	2 to 6 pieces	None	20 - 23 min.**
Meatballs	Fresh	12 pieces	None	18 - 20 min.
Pork chops	Fresh (1 inch thick)	2 to 3 pieces	None	18 - 23 min.**
Pork Tenderloin	Fresh (sliced into ½ inch thick pieces)	1 ¼ lb	1 Tbsp.	12 - 15 min.
Sausages	Fresh	4 to 8	None	10 - 12 min.

Tbsp. = ActiFry spoon

* Yukon Gold recommended - ** Turn halfway through cooking

Times

Fish & Shellfish

	PREPARATION	QUANTITY	OIL	COOKING TIME
Breaded shrimp	Frozen	14 oz bag	None	12 - 16 min.
Shrimp	Cooked, frozen	0.9 lbs	None	10 - 12 min.
Jumbo King Shrimp	Fresh	0.65 lbs	None	13 - 15 min.
	Frozen	16 pieces (0.65 lbs)	None	12 - 14 min.
Tilapia	Fresh in pieces	1.1lbs	1 Tbsp.	20 - 22 min.

Vegetables

	PREPARATION	QUANTITY	OIL	COOKING TIME
Mushrooms	Fresh in quarters	1.4 lbs	1 Tbsp.	12 - 15 min.
Onions	Fresh in rings	1.1 lbs	1 Tbsp.	15 - 25 min.
Sweet peppers	Fresh in slices	1.4 lbs	1 Tbsp. + ⅔ cup cold water	20 - 25 min.
Tomatoes	Fresh in quarters	1.4 lbs	1 Tbsp. + ⅔ cup cold water	10 - 15 min.
Zucchini	Fresh in slices	1.75 lbs	1 Tbsp. + ⅔ cup cold water	25 - 30 min.

Frozen meals

	PREPARATION	QUANTITY	OIL	COOKING TIME
Chili con carne	Frozen	28 oz bag	None	12 - 15 min.
Pasta carbonara	Frozen	28 oz bag	None	15 - 20 min.
Paella	Frozen	28 oz bag	None	15 - 20 min.
Cantonese rice	Frozen	28 oz bag	None	15 - 20 min.
Pan-fried fishand pasta	Frozen	28 oz bag	None	20 - 22 min.
Ratatouille	Frozen	28 oz bag	None	20 - 22 min.

Desserts

	PREPARATION	QUANTITY	OIL	COOKING TIME
Apples	Cut in wedges	3	1 Tbsp. + 1 to 2 Tbsp. of sugar	15 - 18 min.
		6	1 Tbsp. + 1 to 2 Tbsp. of sugar	20 - 25 min.
Bananas	Cut in slices	5 (1.1 lbs)	1 Tbsp. + 1 to 2 Tbsp. of sugar	4 - 6 min.
Cherries	Wholes	Up to 2.2 lbs	1 Tbsp. + 1 to 2 Tbsp. of sugar	12 - 15 min.
Pears	Cut in pieces	Up to 2.2 lbs	1 to 2 Tbsp. of sugar	8 - 12 min.
Pineapple	Cut in pieces	1	1 to 2 Tbsp. of sugar	8 - 12 min.
Strawberries	Cut in quarters or halves	Up to 2.2 lbs	1 to 2 Tbsp. of sugar	5 - 7 min.

recipes in alphabetical order

As part of our customer satisfaction policy,
T-fal offers a Consumer Service Department always ready
to assist you with any questions you may have.
If after all our efforts you are not entirely satisfied with your product,
we invite you to contact T-fal's Consumer Service Department
who will be able to assist you right away.

Our Representatives are available:
Monday through Friday from 8:30am to 5:30pm EST.
Toll free number: **1-800-395-8325**
Internet address: **http://www.t-falusa.com**

Acknowledgements
Ellie Krieger – MS, RD
New York Times Best Selling Author, Food Network Host

SA SEB – 21261 SELONGEY CEDEX – RCS B 302 412 226
Ref : 5086006
All rights reserved

Graphic design and layout:
JPM & Associés

Photo credits:
Image & Associés - Marc Muller - Digital Dimensions - Jacques Blanchard
Melone Advertising Group - Stile (Satinder Bagga) - Fotolia

Production:
Typocentre